MICHELLE WHITEHURST GOOSBY

Order this book online at www.trafford.com
or email orders@trafford.com

Most Trafford titles are also available at major online book retailers.

Note for Librarians: A cataloguing record for this book is available from Library
and Archives Canada at www.collectionscanada.ca/amicus/index-e.html

Printed in Victoria, BC, Canada.

ISBN: 978-1-4269-2756-0

*Our mission is to efficiently provide the world's finest, most comprehensive book publishing
service, enabling every author to experience success. To find out how to publish your book, your
way, and have it available worldwide, visit us online at www.trafford.com*

Trafford rev. 2/3/10

North America & international
toll-free: 1 888 232 4444 (USA & Canada)
phone: 250 383 6864 ✦ fax: 812 355 4082

SAMUEL FARRAND

Dedicated to. . .

My daughter, Jacqueline Michelle
A striking, clever young lady
who gives me the highest form of flattery
by raiding my closets every time she visits.

My son, Gregory Dwight
As I look him in the eye, and say, "You are beautiful."
This handsome, brilliant young man
Turns and replies, "Not as beautiful as you, mom."

My six year old granddaughter, Rosemary Michelle
A precious jewel who carries herself like a princess,
looks like one too and has a mind to match.

My four year old grandson, Aiden Isaiah
A gorgeous little boy who races to open the car door for me
and marvels in saying, "Thank You Grandma."

KAREN DENISE

Dedicated to. . .

My mama and daddy, Martha and Samuel Whitehurst
A faithful, generous twosome who gave me their good genes
and taught me the importance
of humbleness and righteousness.

The memory of my beautiful sister, Karen Denise
Known to everyone as "Niecy"
Beautiful inside and out.

My devoted sister, Muriel Lynett
Who never fails to shower me with gifts and advice.

My loving brother, Samuel Farrand
A walking history book
Conversation with him
Always a fascinating and hilarious experience.

ERIC, KALEB AND MONICA

Dedicated to. . .

My loyal brother, Kevin Keith
Always giving, Always sharing
A pillar of what is and what can be.

My niece and her husband, Monica and Eric
A happy young couple, A sight to behold.

My nephew, Kaleb,
The son of Monica and Eric
My "Little Hank Aaron"
Who hits home runs on the field and in the classroom.

MURIEL AND DADDY

Dedicated to. . .

The memory of Granny, Joella Sanders
The lady who helped us all
And never asked for anything in return
A humanitarian in every sense of the word.

The memory of Grandmama, Martha Diggs
The lady who gave me an extra helping
of her laughter and her genes
A great conversationalist and humorist.

The memory of Granddaddy, Wilbur Tucker
Mathematician, Pianist, and English scholar
A man who danced with the numbers
and whose subjects and verbs
never had a cross word between them.

KEVIN KEITH

Acknowledgements

PHOTOGRAPHY by

Prophetess Lyntresa Williams
A trusted loyal friend and colleague
A constant flow of encouragement and support

Kevin Keith Whitehurst
A dedicated, accomplished young man
who happens to be my brother

TO MY CHURCH AND COMMUNITY
THANK YOU!!

For the prayers, leadership, encouragement and financial support
you have given me throughout my life.

For standing by me eager and willing to assist in
any way that you could
all in the name of saving my life
during my bout with leukemia.

ROSEMARY MICHELLE

CONTENTS

INTRODUCTION

As Blessings Flow Into This Life is a manifestation of my strength, my perseverance, my inspiration, my pain, my humor, my joy and my love. I never forget as I pour my soul into each inspirational line that I am a culmination of Martha and Samuel Whitehurst, my parents. I believe that God gave me the words to share with others.

Nothing short of extraordinary, my testimony goes all the way back to my mother's womb. She almost lost me when she was carrying me; but the Lord saw fit for this bouncing baby girl to enter this world. Since then, it seems I have had this knack for making my presence known to the world, voluntary and involuntary so. As a toddler in the early sixties, after sneaking out of the house with a few pennies in hand to go buy a bag of *two-for-a-penny* cookies from the neighborhood store across the street, I was hit by a car. I was no more than four or five years old. There I was, this little girl, lying in the middle of the road bleeding and gasping for breath. As I lay slumped, breathing heavily in the back seat of a vehicle on its way to Gibson Hospital, I remember mama sitting right beside me crying, it seemed nonstop. I came very close to death. My doctor said that if I had bled on the inside, I would have died. To everyone's dismay, following a brief stint in the hospital due to a slight concussion and a busted eardrum, I was in tip top shape ready to take on the world once again.

As a first grader in 1965 at College Street Elementary School in Enterprise, Alabama I was the only black child in my class, a straight A student, and the talker of the group. Everyone took notice of me and I loved the attention. Constantly, I was ordered by my teachers to stop talking. They then made mama and daddy aware of my shortcomings every six weeks by writing "talks too much" on my report card. I always had something to say it seemed – never at a loss for words. Little did I know that as my life progressed, this habit of "talking too much" would transform itself into a "gift for gab" in tongue and on paper.

In 1975 everybody watched as the enemy stepped into my life with a vengeance. Only sixteen years old, I was stricken with acute lymphocytic leukemia. Interestingly, mama and I had recently attended the funeral of a young girl who died of leukemia without a clue that this unwelcomed guest would soon make its debut in my life. When Dr. Brunson, the attending physician on duty the day I was rushed to the emergency room, informed mama and daddy that I had leukemia, they were devastated and did everything they could to protect me, in particular, my frame of mind. Although my doctor suggested that I be flown to the University Hospital in Birmingham, AL, because they did not want to upset me, mama and daddy dropped everything and transported me there themselves. They refused to tell me anything about my condition until doctors in Birmingham confirmed my illness.

Once the doctors verified my condition, whether I would live or die was anybody's guess, literally. I, on the other hand, never once believed that I would be leaving this world. Somehow I knew I would get better. I lost every strand of my hair, endured numerous blood and platelet transfusions, tolerated daily bouts of chemotherapy and radiation therapy, underwent bone marrows and spinal taps, and suffered with pain, nausea and fatigue. Nonetheless, I knew with certainty that I would be healed and would return to high school.

After months of hospitalization the disease was forced to step aside because death was not in God's plans at that time. My hematologist, Dr. George A. Omura, described my condition as an "extraordinary case". Medically speaking, my condition is in remission; however, I say that I am cured by the grace and mercy of Jesus Christ. Despite it all, in 1977 I graduated from Enterprise High School on time and at the top ten percent of my class. It is clear to me today that my close-to-death experiences served to fuel my drive as a writer allowing me to expand upon fascinating, true-to-form topics as a young adult.

Furthermore, my experience as a student in grade school did much to feed my appetite for speaking. Although I loved mathematics, English revealed itself to be my favorite subject. Using it in verbal and written mode would later become my passion. While attending junior high school and high school, I delved briefly into reciting poetry. I loved reciting poetry in Mrs. Ellisor's seventh grade English class. Joyce Kilmer's *Trees*, and Rudyard Kipling's *If* were among my favorite recitations and she was my favorite teacher at that time. She believed in me and encouraged me. My eighth grade history teacher, Mr. James Crawford, inspired me further with similar assignments. He asked each student to recite the *Preamble to the Constitution* and the *Gettysburg Address*. These recitations remain vivid memories in my mind. They sparked a passion in me that was to rise again and again in my adult life.

My church, Friendship Missionary Baptist Church, further prepared me to be a seasoned writer and speaker. As a child and preteen I constantly found myself reciting scriptures and poetry at church functions. I remember how anxious I was to stand before the congregation and recite *Psalms 100* from memory. Speaking before a crowd with no paper in hand was standard procedure. I was trained by the best youth directors and Sunday school teachers of that time. Youth director, Ms. Doll B. and Sunday School teacher, Mrs. Louise Sconiers were among that elite group. They nurtured my talent as I grew up in that church. They wouldn't let me rest and I loved it. Being well seasoned as a child, I began to write my own speeches such as welcomes, occasions and tributes as a young adult. That was the beginning of an undeniable passion deep within never to let me go.

As time progressed, everything seemed to happen one step at a time. Writing and speaking, my favorite pastimes, consequently, led to my serving as guest speaker and mistress of order for a variety of functions in my community. My church, in particular, my pastor, Dr. J. Henry Williams and First Lady Janice Williams, provided me with a wealth of encouragement by featuring me as speaker at pastor's appreciation events, black history programs and senior citizens tributes. Other community events to include serving as mistress of order for plays written, directed and produced by Bernadette Smith gave me the same type of platform outside the church. It was evident that my love of picking up a pen and lifting my voice to manifest my thoughts was well on its way. I felt as if the Lord had given me wings to fly.

Amidst the writing and public speaking, my love for singing also blossomed in the church, in the community, and in the workplace.As a child I participated in community talent shows and beauty pageants always with a song. Willie Fred Johnson, a neighborhood friend, would prepare contestants who happened to be neighborhood children by holding rehearsals in his grandmother's backyard. As a result at the tender age of nine or ten it was nothingfor me to stand on stage before a crowd and sing my heart out with songs by Gladys Knight, Aretha Franklin and The Staple Singers.

Also, the church and the workplace created opportunities for me to lift my voice with praise. Since Gospel had always been my passion in music, I joined the youth choir as a young girl. Later, as a young adult, I continued to sing and lead songs as a member of The Robinson Chorus and the Mass Choir. Eventually this talent made its way to my workplace and my community. I was also featured as vocalist at college graduations, community talent shows, fundraisers, festivals, funerals and weddings with renditions of Patsy Cline, Gladys Knight and Bette Midler classics. When I think of my singing, I think of how my love for words has manifested itself in song.

My personal life created emotions in me which revealed themselves to be motivational tools in my quest to be a writer. I married at the young age of 18 and within seven years gave birth to two beautiful children, Jacqueline and Dwight. Putting my education on hold as I played the role of housewife and mother was my life. However, after eleven years the marriage was over resulting in my children and me moving back home with my parents. Single with two mouths to feed and unemployed with minimal education, there I stood forced to quickly step up to the plate. I aimed to hit a home run; so I enrolled the three of us in school – Jackie in Head Start, Dwight in elementary school, and Michelle in college. Our lives took off with me at the helm.

A fantastic career ensued with my decision to further my education. Since the numbers and I had always gotten along quite well, mathematics was the best choice for me. Interestingly, as a child I thought nothing of it. After completing my B. S. degree in pure mathematics, I was hired as an adult education instructor for five years. Shortly afterwards, I secured a part time math instructor position in 1996 at Lurleen B. Wallace Community College, known then as Douglas Macarthur Technical College. Three years later I completed an M. S. degree in the same discipline which landed me a fulltime position as a professor of mathematics.

I had not a clue that teaching mathematics was only the beginning of what God had in store for me. Shortly after my career took off, I began to write inspirational poetry – rhymes and rhythmical pieces – during my leisure time. These poetic words were a direct result of ideas and notions that would tend to flood my mind sporadically. With time it became standard procedure for me to write down my thoughts and then later go to my computer to complete those thoughts. This constant venture resulted in my "Thoughts of Michelle" collection. Many of my selections are flavored with a sense of humor I've carried with me throughout my life. Amidst most things that occur in my life, I have got to find a window of laughter. I have got to be able to smile amidst the storm and rain. I have got to share my contentment and passion with the world.

As my "Thoughts of Michelle" collection increased, I decided to venture out, giving the public access to these thoughts. Of course, I would always deliver my literary pieces in my church. In the midst of all of that, something told me I had to go further, bringing my work to the masses. The Southeast Alabama Gazette, owned and operated by Hillard and Ann Hamm, is the route I took to fulfill this goal. Writing a column for this newspaper continually fuels my drive to inspire and motivate others with words. This venture was another stepping stone to what is now and what will be.

Writing and speaking in my mind is a mesmerizing experience, one of the ultimate forms of expression and enjoyment. In hindsight I see that my gift for gab, love for math, and guts to pick up a pen and write have provided me with stability and security in my life. I thank God for the opportunity, the passion, the gifts and the ability. This is my dream. I'm having the time of my life. My wish is for the reader to be inspired and uplifted by these words. I hope that you find them amusing and that they touch your heart in a special way. I desire that you find consolation and validation as you comprehend in your own way what you read. Thank you for inviting me into your lives. My mind tells me that this is only the beginning. So enjoy. There is more to come.

CHAPTER ONE

The Praise and Worship Express. . .

As Blessings Flow Into This Life

To God I humbly kneel and pray
As I proudly walk this earth today.
I reminisce over countless heights
As blessings flow into this life.

So You saved me
From the fast pacing car
Driven by a gentleman unknown
Who hadn't an inkling
That standing idly alone
Midway in the street he was driving down
Was an innocent little girl who appeared spellbound
Unaware she was about to swallow a bitter pill
Administered by a vehicle with him at the wheels.

To God I humbly kneel and pray
As I proudly walk this earth today.
I reminisce over countless heights
As blessings flow into this life.

So You healed me
At the tender age of sweet sixteen,
You gave me a second chance to live
When a blood disease, with a vengeance,
came for my life to steal.
Pain and fatigue, my enemies, kept me company.
Radiation and Chemotherapy,
my friends, turned out to be.
Although it cost me nausea, headaches,
and every strand of my hair,

My hematologist described me
as the patient extraordinaire.

To God I humbly kneel and pray
As I proudly walk this earth today.
I reminisce over countless heights
As blessings flow into this life.

So You protected me
From a vehicle driven by
a woman who had not a clue
That an incoming vehicle
was diligently en route.
Suddenly, I am sideswiped.
I then rollover twice.
Yet I am still breathing and conscious
despite this awful plight.

To God I humbly kneel and pray
As I proudly walk this earth today.
I reminisce over countless heights
As blessings flow into this life.

So You gave me
A mind to think, to analyze,
deduce, and to conclude
Legs to walk complete with two feet
and ten toes to wiggle too.
Arms to hold complete with two hands
and ten fingers to reach out and touch
Eyes to see the beauty of the world,
a mind to see as much
A nose to smell the aromas
be they stench or perfume
A voice to talk, to whisper,
to scream or sing a favorite tune.

To God I humbly kneel and pray
As I proudly walk this earth today.
I reminisce over countless heights
As blessings flow into this life.

I quietly sit and deeply think
About the countless battles I have won.
I meditate over Your goodness Lord.
Overwhelmed, I know more is to come.
I cannot complain when the tide is high
For beyond I can see the sun.
Like a rush, something comes over me.
My work down here is not done.

To God I humbly kneel and pray
As I proudly walk this earth today.
I reminisce over countless heights
As blessings flow into this life.

Linda Michelle Goosby©September 2, 2006
AS BLESSINGS FLOW INTO THIS LIFE

A Teacher's Prayer

Lord, I pray that You give me the Wisdom, Compassion and Expertise to perform my duties as an instructor effectively.

Father, I pray that You give me the ability to relay the subject matter such that each student will leave the session convinced that communication did indeed take place.

Lord, I pray that I will not make assumptions about my students. Remind me to recognize and accept each student for the unique individual that he or she is and the wisdom to know that diversity is such a beautiful thing.

Heavenly Father, allow me to search diligently for the gifts in each student, often times, buried deep within his or her being. Never let me forget that every student is gifted, not just a select few.

Lord, give me the understanding to work with the student who has special needs and the desire to do everything within my ability to accommodate those needs.

Jesus, give me the eyes to see when I am blinded by my status as a teacher and my standing as a member of the community. Keep me well grounded so that I will always put the needs of the student first.

Preparation, Lord, let it take place prior to every session. Remind me constantly that failing to do so puts the learning process of the student in jeopardy.

Laughter, Jesus, Laughter. Give me Laughter. Thank you Sir for doing so. For it is my sense of humor that keeps the energy flowing during each teaching session and the fire burning throughout my teaching career.

Jesus, shower me with charisma so that I may maintain the interest of each student. Lord I want to grasp their attention with a vengeance.

Heavenly Father, adorn me with dedication. I never want to abandon ship. When times get hard and the rain begins to pour, give me the strength to weather the storm, to hold on and never leave my post.

Forgive me Lord when I fall short of my duties for I know that fulfilling my purpose as an instructor should be first and foremost at all times.

Help me Jesus to be diligent in completing my tasks, always, with no exceptions. Father remind me that putting self upfront means putting the student outback. Doing so is not my wish Lord.

Thank You Jesus for giving me the opportunity to make a difference in the lives of the vast number of individuals who cross my path. Thank you Lord, for making me a teacher.

Michelle Whitehurst Goosby©September 21, 2005
A TEACHER'S PRAYER

And He Don't Loan That Thing Out

Nobody on earth wears a halo.
Everybody here is on even keel.
We can all learn from each other.
Get ready, my sister, to swallow that pill.

No need to rant and rave in devastation
No need to brood and pout
For only Jesus wears a halo
And He don't loan that thing out.

Yesterday, as you approached your sister
Looking down your nose at her in dismay,
You never once thought to bestow upon her
A pleasant hello, a smiling face.

Placing yourself above your sister
That is what you are all about.
But only Jesus wears a halo
And He don't loan that thing out.

You know this story well
Jesus loves us one and all.
Yet, you care nothing about your sister
And a Christian, yourself, you call.

It's time for a reality check
As a Christian you don't have no clout
For only Jesus wears a halo
And He don't loan that thing out.

Michelle Whitehurst Goosby©2007
AND HE DON'T LOAN THAT THING OUT

These Words I Live Are Not My Own

These gifts I share
Like the taste of fine wine
These gems I give
They're no creation of mine.

With the snap of a finger
I cannot reproduce
These rubies of consolation
These words of truth

That minister to the weary
That refuse to vacate
The torn weathered soul
Drenched in sorrow and hate.

Like diamonds they sparkle.
Like gold they shine.
The moon in its fullness
Has never been so fine.

You overcome as if
You were under a spell.
Swept away is your pain.
Depression curtailed.

This potion you take
A concoction not mine.
I attribute this to
Someone greater than I.

The good and the sweet,
the pure and the best
That I share with this world
Did not come from this nest.

This medicine I administer
It is not I who prescribes.
A Great Doctor on High
Reigns as the storm subsides.

These words I breath
Will lead and guide me home.
These words I live
Are not my own.

Michelle Whitehurst Goosby©August 2006
THESE WORDS I LIVE ARE NOT MY OWN

Do You Believe It???

Oh, The Happiness of it All
Happier than I have ever been
Since I let Jesus Guide the Course of My Life
Overtaken with Blessings
He keeps on blessing me.
I am driven by the extraordinary Love of Jesus.
Oh to be Loved by Jesus
The Happiness of it all
It is incalculable.
Every bit of trouble that comes my way
Is overshadowed by the Goodness of Jesus.

DO YOU BELIEVE IT???

I think of His Compassion, His Generosity,
His Kindness and His Love.
He is my Consolation
He is the pillar that holds it all together.
The tears I shed,
The pain. The despair,
Temporarily and momentarily make their debut
But I know that Jesus will see me through
it all, for He's done it before.
He's doing it now
And He'll do it tomorrow.
So when it comes, I face it not alone.
He is there by my side holding my hand,
Guiding me and leading me all the way.
I must not forget that.
As He constantly knocks at my door,
"Let Me in. Let Me in. Let Me into your life."
Is the voice I hear.

DO YOU BELIEVE IT???

I say, "Yes, Lord
I love You Lord.
I will be obedient to Your Word."
It is not always easy
Doing the Right thing,
Doing what God would have you to do.
It ain't easy by no means.
It takes work.

DO YOU BELIEVE IT???

Well, you better believe it.
Laziness has no place on this journey.
Dragging around, having no get-up-and-go about yourself
By the time you get out of bed the day is gone.
The opportunity is no longer there.
You've been left behind.

Why the thought of what God has in store for you
Ought to lift you right off of your feet.
It is a rush only an act of God can produce.

And you, Yeah you,
That haughty sister standing at the head of the line
Anxiously waiting for a blessing to come through.
You don't have to wait in line for a blessing.
You simply wait for a blessing.
I don't have to stand behind you
and you don't have to stand behind me.
When the Lord places my name on a blessing, it is mine to keep.
It has nothing to do with you.
When and how I receive it has no relevance
to what others stand to gain.
Just stand and be ready for that instantaneous windfall.

DO YOU BELIEVE IT???

I am so excited about what He has in store for me.
I look forward to living my life
Giving honor to God who has allowed me to grace the world.
I'm thrilled to death.
Oh what a wonderful life
Living my life in the comfort of His arms
I can sleep at night knowing
He's watching over me.
He promised to take care of me,
To never leave me alone.
I believe in Him.
I trust in Him.
I adore Him.

DO YOU BELIEVE IT???

For joy I leap with shoes upon my feet
Food in the frig, a place I call my crib
A fall from grace, As a matter of fact
Yet He gives me a mind with all screws in tack.
For He lifts me up, puts me back together again
Holds me in His loving arms, frees me from all sin.
A choice of clothes to put upon my back
Washed white as snow, my life is on track.

DO YOU BELIEVE IT???

Oh, to be blessed by Jesus
Oh, to be loved by Jesus

I leap for joy.
I twirl with pizzazz.
I walk with a confidence.
Every child of God has.

DO YOU BELIEVE IT???

Michelle Whitehurst Goosby©2009
DO YOU BELIEVE IT?

CHAPTER TWO

The Winds Oh, How They Blow. . .

GREGORY DWIGHT

For She is a Pearl

I look in the mirror. I like what I see.
This beautiful woman glaring back at me.
She looks familiar, her face, her stare.
I know I've seen her before somewhere.

Excited she is, Vibrant, full of life,
Happy and confident, despite the strife
Forced upon her by this despicable world.
Not a worry she has, for she is a pearl.

Suffering, this Lady, surely has been through
Pain and distress, no man can undo.
Manifested through words, a knife deeply cuts.
Healing will come, only if she has the guts

To face her enemy, look him straight in the eye,
For her Heavenly Father stands right by her side.
Brave and confident is this beautiful girl.
Not a worry she has, for she is a pearl.

Her life immersed in joy protects
Her from the perils that life injects
Into her soul but not to stay
For Peace and Harmony push them away.

Love overcomes. Love survives.
Allows her to take it all in stride.
She leaps in elation. Around she twirls.
Not a worry she has, for she is a pearl.

Life's adversities have made her strong.
When you stay prayed up, you can't go wrong.
Her children adore her, Her grandchildren too.
A legacy she leaves with them and who?

The teacher, the preacher, the waitress, the clerk
The doctor, the lawyer, the fool, the jerk
To everyone, this mindset she hurls.
Not a worry she has, for she is a pearl.

I look in the mirror. I like what I see.
This beautiful woman glaring back at me.
She looks familiar. Her face, her stare.
Of course, I've seen her before somewhere.

Alive and vibrant, thanks be to God's Grace.
It is I that I see, face to face.
Drenched in contentment she floats and she swirls.
Not a worry She has, for She is a pearl.

Michelle Whitehurst Goosby©August 2006
FOR SHE IS A PEARL

A Change Of Clothes

You walk in today
Wearing the garments of a lark,
Easy to get along with
Now that the scrooge is in park.

You're in a good mood.
All of your answers are yes.
You're very amenable,
Not bogged down by stress.

You come in another day.
You've had a change of clothes.
Tormented by the world
Why? Nobody knows.

You bite my head off
And proceed to jump down my throat.
My thought at this point,
"Brother please put back on those other clothes."

A third day rolls around.
This time your attire is pure sin.
I think to myself
You've changed clothes again.

You show up a day later,
Calm and serene.
This outfit you're wearing
Is one I've never seen.

I seize this moment to say,
And I don't mean to probe,
"Make this a permanent addition
To your wardrobe."

I sit and think to myself,
"What suit will you wear next?"
"A cloak of delightfulness,
A robe of distress"

Will you show up wearing
Rags of despair
Under a coat of prosperity?
You wouldn't dare.

Wear A gown of excitement
To cover up your sorrows and woes.
Once again it appears
you've had a change of clothes.

Michelle Whitehurst Goosby©August 24, 2006
A CHANGE OF CLOTHERS

Why?? Why?? Why??

Why do you season your life with disgust and dismay?
Why?
Why do you dump your life in the sewer
to be devoured by the dregs of this world?
Why?
Why do you methodically immerse yourself in unsavory company?
Why?
Why do you wear this apparel of self-destruction and self-hate?
Why? Why? Why?

Step out of these scandalous garments.
Throw them away far.
Step into a new suit of wisdom and discernment.
Unveil the beautiful specimen you really are.

Why do you minimize your brother's good
fortune on every end? Why?
Why do you treat your fellowman like a punching bag
when your soul is drenched in woes?
Why?
Why do you waste energy belittling your brother
and downplaying every word he utters?
Why?
Why do you wear these hats
Laced with poisons of self-hatred and malice?
Why? Why? Why?

Rid yourself of these filthy accessories.
Discard them. Set yourself free.
Wash your hands of it all.
Put on a headdress of encouragement and responsibility.

Why do you complain like it is the best
thing since chocolate cake? Why?
Why do you jump to the plate to take credit for something good
when ownership is in the hands of another?
Why?
Why do you hide behind a curtain of shame
when something bad, handcrafted by you
is brought to the forefront? Why?
Why do you wear these cloaks of bitterness,
shiftiness and deceitfulness?
Why? Why? Why?

Step out of these grimy clothes.
Wash them in bleach? You'd better not think!
Bury them six feet under instead.
Make them history. Don't even blink.

Why do you stump a thunderstorm
on your sister's moment of sunshine?
Why?
Why do you dance a jig around your sister's demise?
Why?
Why do you run and take cover leaving your
sister all alone in the dark? Why?
Why do you walk in these shoes
of jealousy, insecurity and cowardliness?
Why? Why? Why?

Shake loose these venomous shackles.
Toss them in the furnace. Burn them to a crisp.
Loose these toxic chains.
Step into a tidal wave of fresh air now in the midst.

Michelle Whitehurst Goosby©December 29, 2006
WHY?? WHY?? WHY??

Confessions
of The Ignorant Intellectual

My degrees! See them hanging on the wall.
This, of course, means I have arrived.
I've got these pieces of paper, you see.
This indisputable fact they verify.

I know more than the average person.
Broken English, I do not use.
I come from a good family.
That makes me better than you.

My doctorate, my masters,
My position, they speak for themselves.
I am a pillar of society.
Everyone in town knows me well.

My bank account is bottomless.
My vehicle and my home can attest.
My children never give me any trouble.
Their worst is your children's best.

As you stroll past me,
I wouldn't dare part my mouth to speak.
To even think of doing such a thing,
It is beneath me, you see.

I profess to be a Christian
Because I pay my tithes.
I go to Church on Sunday.
I even sing in the choir.

Many have asked me this question,
Who do you think you are?
Looking down your nose at us,
With your designer clothes and fancy cars.

Well, I am the ignorant intellectual.
You will find me far and near.
I am so high and mighty
I cannot see my way clear.

In order, my priorities are not.
Missing out on the better things in life.
Believing I can buy happiness and
My way out of strife.

I lack humility and compassion.
Precious jewels from my past.
I conned myself into placing
Material things first and not last.

As I prepare for my departure
It's clear these gloves don't fit.
So then I reach for a hat.
On my head, I attempt to place it.

I struggle with this task,
A test I'm sure to fail.
Attempting to place a hat
On a head that has swelled.

My status, my power, my wealth
I thought defined me well.
But my character, corrupt and twisted,
Has landed me at the fiery gates of Hell.

Michelle Whitehurst Goosby©January 27, 2007
CONFESSIONS OF THE IGNORANT INTELLECTUAL

Why I Smile

Thrown In the midst of adversity,
I suffer and yet I smile.
The pain thrust upon me by the hardship of living
hits me on every end, deeply piercing me in the side.
With a fist to my face it knocks me down.
I get back up and I stand tall.
Ferociously grabbing me from behind,
it drags me to the ground.
It proceeds to kick me to and fro.
I quickly turn with a smile.

Inflicting pain is its greatest desire.
Repeatedly taunting me with its actions and words,
The words rolling off of its lips
smother me time and time again.
Yet, I continue to breath.
Like a thief in the night
It comes and snatches my peaceful slumber.
I cry out as I awaken wreaking with joy despite it all.
My screeching voice may mirror the suffering I endure.
Nonetheless, I continue to move forward by the grace of God.
I do it all with a smile.

My heart is heavy.
Yet, my soul is at rest.
Although many times I feel worn and torn,
I continue to withstand life's wear and tear.
The Lord said in his word
that he would make my enemies my footstool.
Why should I fear? Whom shall I fear?
After all, a footstool serves only to lift me up.
My Heavenly Father is watching over me
and I find peace in the comfort of His arms.

So yes I smile.
The atrocity life thrusts upon me has warped its vision
such that all it can see is my stream of tears,
My agony and constant pain brings it pleasure.
Yet amidst this travail, it has not touched me.
Bamboozled is it.
Despite its attempts to destroy my soul.
My happiness is constant and ever flowing,
My gush of peace and prosperity,
My ever flowing love,
It keeps coming and coming.
"How can this be?"

I will tell you why.
Because it is incapable of going behind the scene,
It will never discern my unspeakable bliss
and peace of mind,
For it must receive it to comprehend it.
Unless it does, it will always be lurking in the dark,
Functioning under a cloud of confusion,
Exhausting its energies
While focusing on the destruction of another.

Oh yes, I fight back
But I don't dare retaliate with an assault.
I don't lift a finger to hurt it.
I don't spit in its face nor do I knock it down.
Inflicting pain is not my game.
And yet I'm winning this war.
Amidst all that is not said and all that is not done
I am the stronger and I am the bigger.
It hits and misses, plots and schemes,
A futile task as I quietly pray.
For a Mighty Warrior is my God
Is why I smile at the end of day.

Michelle Whitehurst Goosby@August 10, 2006
WHY I SMILE

The Lesson of the Gutter

Though I dwell in the gutter a little while, this is not my home.
The gutter is not a place where I wish to set up residence.
It is merely a place that I visit from time to time.
Involuntarily so! And not too often! I never enjoy my stay.
I never forget I've been there. I don't wish to go back.
And I don't care for visitors.
But once they get there, I say come on in and stay a little while.
Nonetheless, I draw strength from my visit there.
It has taught me many lessons. Thanks be to God.

You see, I don't plan to waste my time there.
Yet, it seems many others are quite comfortable there,
Wallowing in the sludge of self-pity,
Consumed with the fiery blaze of wrath,
All wrapped up in the constraints of hopelessness and despair,
Letting their grudge be their master.
Unlike they, I have no plans to drown in
this quick sand of desolation.

You laugh thinking you have gotten the best of me.
Ha! Gutter you have taught me well.
I take this opportunity to reap a harvest
Unbeknownst to you and your tenants.
I get up, pack my bags, and go north
Never to return to this barren land.

With the twinkling of an eye, I disappear.
Ha! Look who is laughing now.
I go with the wind. Quicker than quick!
I make my way out of this hell-hole you prepared just for me.
Plans have changed. My time with you has been cut short.
I am no longer your slave. Don't you see.
The drudge of the night has released me.

This isn't the way it was meant to be.
Don't go looking for me either.
You will never be able to grasp my spirit again.
Your slave has been delivered from bondage. Ha!
I reach for the star of joy and hope.
I reach for the star of humility and strength.
It is within my reach. There it is.
It has been there all the time.
God put it there just for me.
With a firm grip I grab hold.

Blinded by circumstance, I could not see.
Now guess what is in my possession.
Freedom! Oh How the Lord Takes Care of Us!
Thank you Jesus for giving me this second chance.
Thank you for saving my life.

My heart, as it beats uncontrollably,
deep within begins to flutter.
For you took the time, Jesus Christ, to teach
The Lesson of the Gutter.

Michelle Whitehurst Goosby©August 2006
THE LESSON OF THE GUTTER

The Sea of Music

As I ride its waves,
I think to myself
"Oh, how my heart is captured by its spirit."
My soul is drenched in its warm embrace.
My mind ensures that it will always be with me.
My ears allow me to pick and choose
that which is pleasant and satisfying,
that which is breathtaking and riveting.

I have not authorized society to do such.
Though you are free to give your opinion, of course,
I will listen, but I shall not be swayed.
My heart directs my ears and overrides my mind.
It keeps me coming back time after time after time.
My soul is consumed with it.
I cannot let it go. It is a part of me.

I plunge myself into the rapids of this raging sea
and find a place I call home.

Streams of consolation and peace run rampantly
as I submerge myself into its still waters.
Bottomless it is, never running dry,
Forever drenching my soul,
A perpetual antidote for my sorrows and woes,
So consoling, what am I to do?
But to constantly immerse myself into its waters
Morning, noon and night.

Its waves toss me to and fro.
I wade in it. I bathe in it. I drown in it.
I never want to come up for breath.
I sip it.I gulp it. I live it. I breath it.

When I am troubled, I go there for solace.
When I am happy, it is the place I wish to be.
When I am sad, it speaks my mind and keeps me company.
When I am torn, it settles my case.
When my mind is made up, it confirms my choice.

Inundated by its power
It moves me. It soothes me. It calms me. It tantalizes me.
It swings me from left to right.
It shakes me. It breaks me.
It makes me. It takes me.

I am reduced to streams of tears.
I am elevated to unspeakable delight.
I am moved to and fro
From countless lows to countless heights.
Only silence of the mind can rid me of it. Or can it?
It will always be with me.

Oh Lord, I thank You for this gift of which I cannot get enough.
Tell me. Who would not want to drink of this cup?

Michelle Whitehurst Goosby©July 23, 2006
THE SEA OF MUSIC

This Is A Thing That Mankind Does!

Take a good look at what has been and is.
Watch the web of life unwind.
This is a thing that mankind does.
Yet man is not always kind.

The destructive, agonizing thing in this life
Inflicted down under and up above
Is indicative of one and only one group.
This is a thing that mankind does.

Not a thing that a certain nationality does,
Not a thing that a certain race does,
Not a thing that a certain gender does,
Not a thing that a certain faith does,

Not a thing that the impoverished one does,
Not a thing that the wealthy does,
Not a thing that the sensible one does,
Not a thing that the foolish one does,

Not a thing that the ignorant one does,
Not a thing that the intelligent does,
Not a thing that the beautiful one does,
Not a thing that the unsightly one does,

You can't pin this on a certain group
It does not discriminate.
Humanism is all you need to qualify
For wickedness to escalate.

Man has been categorized by religion,
denomination, wealth, and race,
sexual preference, gender,
intelligence, model and make.

Don't put me in a your little box
Don't place me on a paper plate
For evilness makes its way through all walks
By no means, does this thing discriminate.

Michelle Whitehurst Goosby©2008
THIS IS A THING THAT MANKIND DOES

CHAPTER THREE

When I Think Of You. . .

A TRIBUTE TO
MAMA AND DADDY

MARTHA AND SAMUEL WHITEHURST

When I Think of Jesus. . .

When I think of Jesus,
I think of His Grace and His Mercy.
I think of His Undying, Unconditional Love.
I think of His Goodness, His Kindheartedness, His Compassion.
I think of His Humbleness, His Meekness, and His Holiness.
I think of the miracle of His birth and the Mother Mary.
I think of this little baby boy
who had not a place to lay His precious little head.
I think of this brave young man
who was always about His Father's Work.
I think of how He healed the sick and raised the dead.
I think of His suffering and His pain.
I think of how He never said a mumbling word.
I think of how He died on that old rugged cross,
was buried in a borrowed grave
and how He got up early that Sunday morning.
I think of how He prayed, "Not My Will but Thy Will Be Done."

I think of, as the old folks say,
"the reasonable portion of my health and strength."
I think of how He saved my soul.
I think of this constant flow of joy
that the world cannot lay claim to.
I think of the beautiful years I've lived
and the beautiful years I'm living
all because of His great sacrifice.
I think of how He tucks me in bed every night
and how He watches over me as I sleep.

I think of how He steps in and swoops me up just in time
when disease like a thief in the night tries
to snatch my breath away.
I think of how He puts shoes on my feet and clothes on my back

when nothing but hangers adorn the racks in my closet.
I think of how He without fail gives me sense enough to know
how to get up and go about my everyday activities.

I think of how He adorns me with readiness
to take on the world and all of the ugliness it has to offer.

I think of how He paints a smile on my face
when I've spent all day sobbing
because the world mistook me for a punching bag.

I think of how He pays my bills when my pockets are bare
and my bank account needs refueling.

I think of how He lifts my spirits to great heights
when my heart is heavy and family and friends
are incapable of understanding my pain.

I think of how He guides me and leads me
when I am wondering around idly trying to find my way home.

I think of how He comes to my rescue in the twinkling of an eye
when I am out of a job, out of money and
out of a place to call home.

I think of how He picks me up and puts me back together again
when the love of my life has broken my heart into a million pieces.

I think of how He holds my hand as I stumble in the dark
trying to make it through life's crossing.

I think of how He eases my pain as I walk mile after mile
on hot coals in this wilderness.

I think of how He hides me in His loving arms
when the perils of life try to obliterate me.

I think of how He breathes life in me and tells old death
"Mind your manners." when doctors have just told me
"Pack your bags, you're going south."

I think of how He forgives and continues to love little ole me
when I have neither the fortitude nor the gumption it takes
to abide in His Mighty Word as I'm tossed and turned
by the winds and the rains of this life.
I think of how He thwarts the enemy by wrapping me in His Word
as the enemy unsuccessfully attempts to steal my joy
and drag me down into the gutters of the ungodly
where all manner of evilness prevails.

I think of how He turned water into wine and
how He then transformed my cold heart
into a clean loving vessel drenched in His Word.

I think of this man, the Keeper of My Soul.
I think of His Sovereignty, how He can do anything He wants to do.
I think of how God gave Him to you and me.

I think of
His Birth, His Life, His death, His resurrection
His Love, His Humbleness, His Spirit, His Purpose
I will never forget this man born of a virgin
I will always love this man, the Son of God
who was always about His Father's Work.
Because of His Grace and His Mercy,
Eternal Life is at our Fingertips.

Michelle Whitehurst Goosby©December 18, 2009
When I Think of Jesus

The Seasoned Entrée of Life
A TRIBUTE TO SENIORS

With a host of years, wisdom, fine lines to claim
I make my debut come shine or rain.

And God I thank You, for the joy and pain.
For what life dished out should have left me insane.

You say you wonder from whence I came.
"A drop of longevity, my permanent stain"

Please do me the honor. Hand me my cane.
As we stroll hand in hand down memory lane.

My dwindling health, no one do I blame,
For I woke this morning with a functional brain.

Blessings from God, He'll do you the same.
Obedience to Him, Let us strive to maintain.

So I made some mistakes driving in the fast lane.
I lend my hand to you brother. My living's not in vain

And so be it, a while have I been on this train.
With honor I arrive, from complaints I refrain.

All you got to do is live to enter this domain.
The Seasoned Entrée of Life, my claim to fame

Dodging life's bullets enabled me to gain
Undying love, peace of mind. Need I explain?

Strength and contentment, I walk with this cane.
God's gifts to a soldier, my life over He reigns.

My child don't you see what God has ordained.
My sister just look what I have attained.
I've traveled great years on this passenger train.
I've suffered a day many, yet have I no disdain.

Come courage or fear, come shine or rain.
Let us all celebrate. Bring out the champagne.

With a host of years, wisdom, fine lines to claim
Stand tall with honor, from complaints refrain.

Through years of praise and worship, this I ascertain
Give God all the glory. Praise His Holy Name.

Michelle Whitehurst Goosby©May 1, 2009
THE SEASONED ENTRÉE OF LIFE

That's My Daddy

A TRIBUTE TO DADDY

You spend your life making a living for us all.
You work your fingers to the bones.
You are the Head of the Household.
You stand proud and strong.
Many times you have to leave us,
me, mama, brother and sister all alone.
You sacrifice your time on the job
to say one day this house I own.
You struggled, took mess off of people,
to make this house a home.
"That's my daddy!" I proudly say,
"Give me that microphone!"

Your love for me, brother and sister by everyone is known.
You spank our behinds, so we have sense enough
to know the right from the wrong.
You taught us to work hard. That is always your tone.
You believe in God's Word; now we sing that song.
"That's my daddy!" I proudly say,
"Give me that microphone!"

You keep food on the table
so we can grow up healthy with strong bones.
And you always have change in your pocket
for candy or an ice cream cone.
If anybody messes with me, brother and sister,
You say "Leave my child alone!"
You make us do our homework. You yell,
"Get off that telephone!"
"That's my daddy!" I proudly say,
"Give me that microphone!"

Michelle Whitehurst Goosby©2009
THAT'S MY DADDY

An Angel Called Nurse

I come in pain and discomfort.
For a healing touch I come in search.
I cry for hands to put my life in.
God sends an Angel called Nurse.

In full armor comes an Angel,
A Forever Radiant Bright Star.
A Soldier in constant battle
Fighting for Life in this war.

You're the Someone who brought comfort
To my Child, you gave your hand.
Treating mind as well as body
With medicine not made by man.

Standing by him constantly,
Wiping droplets of tears away,
Your words, your smile, your tender touch,
Warms the passing of the day.

When I think of that Someone
Who steps into this wonderful life,
Someone who takes care of little ole Me,
As I struggle in pain throughout the night.

You take the time to identify,
To nurture my countless needs.
Be they physical or mental
Everyday you constantly feed.

When I think of that someone
Beyond the call of duty, traveling afar
Just to give Father a helping hand,

God's Angel is what you are.
Someone who stood by like a soldier
To lift his spirits, you took the time.
Someone who checked on his wellbeing,
You will always come to mind.

You cannot know the comfort and peace
You bring amidst the constant tide,
For throughout dear Sister's healing.
With my family you laughed and cried.

My heart is heavy and aches as I
Helplessly watch Mother suffer.
My burst of joy overwhelms as I
Witness your being there for her.

I know God will see us through.
He sends Angels to help along the way.
When our good health and mighty strength,
Before our very eyes goes astray.

An even when they cannot find
Their weary way back home,
Your aura of wisdom and solace
Remind that we are never alone.

I kneel and pray when I think
Of One as special as You.
Please God continue to guide
What your Call leads You to do.

I come in pain and discomfort.
For a healing touch I come in search.
I cry for hands to put my life in.
God sends an Angel called Nurse.

Michelle Whitehurst Goosby©2009
AN ANGEL CALLED NURSE

The Irreplaceable Grandparent

Allow me, Your Grandchild, To Do The Honors.
Granny, Grandpa, Big Mama, Big Daddy, Grandmama, Mimi,
Mima, Honey, Papa Jack, Granddaddy, Grandmother,
Grandfather, Granddad, Nana
As I reminisce over life's journey,
I find a Feast for thought.

Thank you for showing me that my life would be nothing
without the grace and mercy of Jesus Christ.
Thank you for that special attention that you give me
every time you see me.
Thank you for loving me unconditionally, no strings attached.
Thank you for scolding me, standing up for me
and supporting me when I was wrong.

Thank you for taking care of me
when mama and daddy were not around to do the honor.
Thank you for all the times you took me in, fed
me, and clothed me, when daddy and mama were
busy trying to make a living for us all.
Thank you for giving me a place to stay
when mama and daddy kicked me out of the house
because I didn't have sense enough to know
that my attitude needed a major adjustment.

Thank you for the good genes that you passed on to mama and
daddy, who then passed them on to me ensuring that I would be
the beautiful person that I am today, inside and out.
Thank you for raising me when mama and daddy could not,
and sometimes would not.
Thank you for being my mother and father, when the Lord chose
to take my mama and daddy away when I was just a child.
Thank you for giving me a mama and daddy

who loves me and cares for me.

Thank you for every prayer you prayed, every tear you cried and
every moment of sleep you lost worrying about my wellbeing.
Thank you for the hugs and kisses that you still give me
even though I am fully grown.

Thank you for all of the material things too, the clothes, the shoes,
the money for college, the purchase of my senior portraits,
need I say more. Well, I think I'd better.
Thank you for paying my bills when you didn't have to,
my electric bill, my water bill, my credit card bill. . .
Thank you for cosigning when I purchased my first car.

Thank you for making my car payment last month.
Whom am I fooling?
Thank you for making my car payment every month
without giving it a second thought when I had no means to do so.
Thank you for believing in me, having faith in me,
trusting me, inspiring me, encouraging me.
Thank you for taking up for me
despite what mama and daddy and everybody else had to say
when you and I both knew I was wrong.
Thank you for seeing something good in me
that nobody else could see, sometimes not even mama and daddy.

Thank you for having the foresight to see that the person
who was crossing my path meant me no good.
You said, "Get rid of that so and so!" and I did it.

Thank you for showing me how cool it is to grow old, in particular,
all of the senior citizens benefits I can look forward to,
the free tea at fast food restaurants and
the discounts at department stores.
Thank you for showing me that it is okay to throw my
weight around sometimes when I reach a certain age,
just like you did that hot summer day, granny,

when you and I were standing in the back of a long line
outside the court house waiting to get your car tag renewed.
Remember how you marched, with your walking cane in hand
and me with you, to the front of the line exclaiming to the others,
"I am a senior citizen." I was so embarrassed, but
I didn't say a word. I let you do the talking.

A Word of Advice to All
Love your grandparents while they are still around.
Spend time with them. Draw from their wisdom.
They have lived a long time, at least longer than you.
They have many beautiful, colorful, humorous,
delightful, chilling, stories to tell.
Listen and Inquire.
Let them know that they are important to you.
Remember they are partially responsible for your being here
with God's help, of course. God helped them along the way.
You are an extension of them. It is a fact. And you
cannot change it. Oh what a wonderful gift God
has given you. Don't you ever forget it.

Granny and Grandpa,
We thank God for giving you a special place in our lives and
in our hearts. You are the rainbow of love that adorns the
family package. Thank you for all of those little extras and
extraordinary moments you've given us. Thank you for the big
ones too. Because of your specialty, that is, being a grand parent,
we recognize you for the beautiful people you are.
Thank you for giving me the honor of going down in history as
Your Grandchild.
Thank You Lord for giving me this Gift of Love.

Michelle Whitehurst Goosby©September 9, 2006
THE IRREPLACEABLE GRANDPARENT

Harriet Tubman Was Her Name!

A God – Fearing woman!
A phenomenal woman!
A tough woman! A clever woman!
A brilliant woman! A courageous woman!
A drop-dead gorgeous woman!
Harriet Tubman was her name.

This woman was phenomenal.
She was a humanitarian of the highest kind.
She was a soldier in the army of human rights
Fully armed with ammunition that only an exceptional mind
Could maneuver and detonate.
Harriet Tubman was her name.

This woman was brilliant.
Her mission in life unfolded right before the eye of mankind.
She developed a strategic plan which led to
the exodus of hundreds of the oppressed and the suppressed.
She built a railroad to freedom
With her own mind and hands.
Fulfillment of her mission manifested itself as a train
Fueled with the blood, sweat, tears and joy of humankind.
The enemy had a deaf ear to the train whistle
As she cried out for freedom and got it.
Harriet Tubman was her name.

This woman was tough.
Weariness, fatigue, fear and pain
Served as inoperative deterrents of her mission.
All too familiar with these feelings she was,

For her entire life was drenched in the same.
Harriet Tubman was her name.

This woman was courageous.
She took great risks to rescue her own and yours alike,
Fully aware that each step she took
Brought with it a stamp of probable death.
She boldly walked into the face of suffering, pain and despair
as she answered to a higher calling.
Harriet Tubman was her name.

This woman was clever.
She looked beyond the color barrier and
discovered a network of allies to help her along the way.
Hiding from the enemy was one of many maneuvers she mastered
And maintained while steps ahead of the game.
Her dedication and loyalty to the cause
took precedence over helplessness and hopelessness,
places she'd never tarry,
that dare try to still her joy and drive.
She led mine and yours to a place called freedom.
Harriet Tubman was her name.

This woman was drop-dead gorgeous.
Her presence alone demanded the utmost respect,
A tower of esteem that preceded her every move.
Her very essence would stop you dead in your tracks.
Anyone who'd dare try to put her efforts to a halt
can appropriately be described as an
ignoramus of the lowest kind.
Stunning she was. Stunning she is.
Her beauty lies within her drive, her determination, her
remarkable labors for the Black slave, for humankind.
Harriet Tubman was her name.

She bore children. She bore the lash.
She shed tears. She smiled. She laughed.
She struggled. She slept. She got up. She fought.
Through it all Freedom was bought.
Harriet Tubman was her name.

Michelle Whitehurst Goosby©2007
HARRIET TUBMAN WAS HER NAME

The Pink Lady

A TRIBUTE TO MARISSA

A beautiful young woman named Marissa
Has graced the world with her presence another year.
The Lady in Pink has appeared on the scene
With all of her faculties in full gear.

The Pink Lady has unsurprisingly made it through.
Twenty spectacular years have passed and gone.
She's grown up, ready to face this volatile world
In full uniform, audacious, and strong.

So young and spree, like a sprinter she races
With no plans to stop until she makes it to the finish line.
She will not quit until she reaches the icy top
Of the snow capped mountain she tediously climbs.

The Pink Lady must courageously face the fears
That the world requires of her life.
Nevertheless, the joy and happiness she anticipates
Make all the pain and strife worthwhile.

You see, the Pink Lady answers to a higher authority
Who endowed her with this beautiful life.
He died on the cross that she might live
The Son of God, her Savior, Jesus Christ.

One step further on this journey she has taken
As she battles through the wind and rain.
She realizes as she meticulously tunnels through
Numerous victories are hers to claim.

She stands up for herself and is willing to fight.
No matter what befalls her or what be the test.
Just take one glance inside her beautiful life,
You'll see The Pink Lady is immensely blessed.

Michelle Whitehurst Goosby©October 8, 2006
THE PINK LADY

The Blooming of the Blossom

A TRIBUTE TO TINA

A Seed of God ready to take on joy and pain
I stepped onto this weary land.
Despite it all I grew into this beautiful blossom
With just one stroke of my Father's Hand.
I've been on this train a long long time
Crying and screaming, yet praying I beat death.
Said the Lord in stride "Old death behave."
When doctors thought I had taken my last breath.

Wracking my brain trying to figure it all out
"Why am I forced to weather this stormy sea?"
I ain't got no time to sit here and pout
For Oh Lord You're watching over me.

The enemy comes in many forms
I think as I go through dialysis.
I clearly see a stepping stone to gain
For Lord, you have the final analysis.

Thank you Jesus I say again and again
As I humbly bend down on my knees.
I pray for good health and mighty strength
And suddenly my pain begins to ease.

Keep coming, they keep coming, Oh Lord
These Blessings from Heaven above.
Keep running, keep me running, Oh Lord
This race fueled with your precious Love.

I am a fighter, my Lord, not a quitter.
Can't let anything hold me back.
I am grateful, my Lord. not bitter.
Father, I know You're on my track.

I worked so hard all of my life.
I made mistakes while on this trail.
Forgive me, Oh Lord, for my every sin
Stumbling blocks, please Lord curtail

You gave me a second chance in life.
I will forever praise Your name.
You are my sole provider Lord.
Eternal Life I stand to gain.

The Blooming of the Blossom, I pray my Lord
Nurtured by your mercy and grace.
From now on, all the days of my life
To Your throne Lord, I will make haste.

Michelle Whitehurst Goosby© November 2009
THE BLOOMING OF THE BLOSSOM

The City of Enterprise Kneels Down to Pray

An Intruder, so unlikely, A violation of a small town,
A Community exasperated, Not a dry eye can be found.

Hearts shattered, Minds boggled, Leaving
Frayed Weathered Souls.
A Massive Devastation forced upon the Young and Old.

It came as if with a vengeance, An act with God at the controls.
Winds with speeds unimaginable, Chilling stories forever told.

Trees snapped, uprooted, Vehicles tossed
like toothpicks to and fro.
Buildings toppled, Houses crumbled, Desolation served to go.

Lives taken without notice, Lives broken without a clue.
Loved ones at perfect peace, Consolation for me and you.

Lives swept away within seconds, But then God is in the plan.
There lies a message for each Courageous woman and man.

Putting pieces back together, precious lives never the same.
Terror faced, pain suffered, stepping stones to gain.

Tears of agony, Streams of joy, Floods of Heavy laden hearts.
Tired, battered, weathered souls see a bright and shining star.

A land of milk and honey prepared just for you and me.
An eternal resting place, Cherished souls are set free.

Don't question God's actions. Learn to accept and believe.
Desolation and Destruction, if you live, you must receive.

Joy cometh in the morning after weeping for a night
God will bring you out of darkness and into His Glorious Light.

A city broken yet grateful, heads bowed down, on its knees,
Prays fervently for its Children, "Don't pass me by, Savior please."
The City of Honor comes together.
The City of Valor does whatever it takes.
The Wellbeing of its Residents,
A Top Priority it makes.

The City of Strength makes its statement,
aware that Healing is underway.
The City of Enterprise, Alabama
Humbly Kneels Down to Pray.

Michelle Whitehurst Goosby©March 8, 2007
THE CITY OF ENTERPRISE KNEELS DOWN TO PRAY

A Message to a Grieving Son

Your heart is heavy and His soul is at rest.
A bitter pill it is to swallow. A drink you could not refuse to take.
You ask, "Lord, why have You served me this cocktail?"
Someone very special in your life has been taken.
Whiffed away to a better place
A place where peace reigns, joy, contentment,
and love on every end
A place you plan to go to one day
A place that God in all His glory has prepared for His children
You knew this day was coming.
And yet your soul was not prepared for your father's departure.
You shed a river of tears and your heart shattered into pieces
As you watched him suffer day after day,
week after week, month after month.
It tore you apart to watch him
as he helplessly endured excruciating pain.
You did all you could for him. You were there for him.
You took care of him. You loved him deeply despite everything.
You forgave him and you know that he forgave you.
You wish often that you could turn back the hands of time
And see him again in all of his strength, vibrancy, and stamina.
You long to have conversation with him,
laugh with him, pray with him.
This unbearable pain he suffered, it is now gone.
And you thank God for taking his hurt away.
He told you that he loved you as he quietly departed your life.
You told him that you loved him too.
He was your father and his well being was always
of the utmost importance.
He was the man responsible for bringing you into this world.
You are forever a part of him and He is forever a part of you.
Nothing can change that.
And you wouldn't have it any other way.

Jesus, I thank you for the time you gave me with my father."
Thank you for allowing me to bond with this man
during his last days on this earth.
Thank you for the peaks and valleys, the bitter and the sweet
Thank you Heavenly Father for showing me
that living is what life is really worth.

Michelle Whitehurst Goosby©2007
A MESSAGE TO A GRIEVING SON

CHAPTER FOUR

*Yours Truly,
Michelle. . .*

The Symphony

My entire life is at my disposal. It is a symphony well orchestrated by the touch of my hand. Oh yes, I am the maestro. My Master has appointed me as such. If I expect to fulfill my responsibility as his servant, I must drink from the cup of preparation. Is it not my desire to take great care in composing my music and fine-tuning my instruments? I must make haste for the Kingdom of Heaven is at hand. I plan to go there one day, you see, to be with my Master. My love for Him surpasses any earthly love I could possibly experience. When this life is over, my place will be with Him.

This is my Life! The Symphony!

The melodies I produce will ultimately become my biography. And rightly so! For I am the composer. However, only my Master knows the real me. Though others will be fooled into thinking that they know me well, time will reveal that their ideas of me are merely a façade. After all, it is I who writes the music and not they. Music indeed! Why, harmony will flow in and out of my life like a constant stream. Then slowly emerging out of diligence and dedication will be a smooth flowing melodic tune, a sonata. Not without conditions, of course. You see, every good decision that I make, if you will, is an instrument fine-tuned. But even so, I must still hit the right notes at the right times for my life to come into focus. I need your wisdom, Heavenly Father! My first composition is completed!

This is My Life! The Symphony!

Each and every waking moment that I spend with my Heavenly Father is precious in His sight. Every prayer that I pray, Every Word of God that I read and every ounce of faith that I possess has its purpose. You must understand that these are the tools that I use to fine-tune each instrument in my orchestra. On a happy note, there will be peace in the valley. I will never cease to thank my Lord for these times. On a sad note, there will be war on the home-front. I will thank my Lord for these times as well. They serve only to make me stronger as his servant.I will not sway. For these things are pleasing in my Lord's sight. Amidst it all, I will not fail to fall down on my knees, receive his Holy Word, and sing praises to His name. Praise you, my Lord! Another composition is completed.

This is My Life! The Symphony!

I am well aware that throughout my performance the tempo will change. Fast paced one moment, slow-paced the next, low notes in the evening, high notes in the morning, crescendo today, decrescendo tomorrow! I know these things will come to be. Suddenly, I will find myself overwhelmed with exhaustion, but my work, Lord, is it complete? Am I destined to do more.? Give me strength Wonderful Counselor! One more composition is completed!

This is My Life! The Symphony!

Surely, the time and effort put forth in the composition and performance of my beautiful sonata, my diligence and dedication, my heartache and pain will not go unnoticed. Certainly, my work will be rewarded. I am confident of this. Oh, Prince of Peace, this I ask of You, keep me day by day. My final composition is completed!

I am weak and tired now.
It seems my day is coming to a close.
This is the End! And yet this is the Beginning!
The Masterpiece Unfolds!

2002©Michelle Whitehurst Goosby
THE SYMPHONY!

From the Depth of a Teacher's Soul

THE GUESTS OF HONOR!!!

The door bell rings and I know who stands on the other side waiting for an answer. I have waited anxiously for their arrival. I have exhausted much of my energy in preparation for this event. This is a come-as-you-are affair. There is no respect of person here. Everyone is on even keel. As a matter of fact, I would not have it any other way. I count the opportunity to provide a service for ones such as these an honor and a pleasure. My answer is "Please come in and be seated. The show is about to begin. A special place has been reserved just for you. Dinner will be served momentarily." As the vast many cross my path, I am constantly reminded of the role I play in the molding of the satisfying and prosperous lives of ones such as these, the Guests of Honor.

As I gaze at the fresh faces of those who walk through that door, I am reminded of my purpose and my decision to implement such a purpose. In doing so, my heart and my mind make a pact to fulfill my desirous obligations as I ponder over the worthiness of a group such as this. I am in awe of these members of society who have decided to tax their brains with the bombardment of knowledge and know-how that I dump on their plate of life. I embrace their thirst for knowledge, their curiosity, their doubts, their fears, their exuberance, their apathy. I admire them for the undeniable courage and unwavering sacrifice displayed as they tackle such a challenge. Heaven forbid me to stand in their way. They are the guests of honor and they will be treated as such. It is my wish that they feel welcome and that from this day forward they feel free to come back for another round. Driven, to say the least, that is who I am, constantly striving to make a difference in the lives of ones such as these.

I have a special menu planned for these honored visitors. I vow to be cognizant of the brand of knowledge I serve and the manner in which I serve it, as I am reminded constantly that it is these things that can make or break the learning process of ones such as these. Because I don't want anyone to leave empty handed, changes to my menu must be made from time to time in an effort to satisfy the ever changing hunger of these who sit at my table. Although the food for thought that I dish out may be bitter to the taste at times, it later proves to be a savory lesson in the school of life. Therefore, serve it, I will. It is my aspiration that ones such as these depart from this venture with the essential tools that will allow them to tunnel through another phase in this chapter of their lives.

My purpose for the vast many who have come my way – passersby, if you will, who stop by for just a little while to get their fill of knowledge – is for them to leave with something in hand that will assist in the enjoyment of life's journey. When my guests cross the threshold of their calling, I want them to do so with a piece of paper in hand, a beautiful smile on the face and an embodiment of skills to match. The door bell rings and I know who stands on the other side waiting for an answer. I open the door and what to my twinkling eyes should appear but an array of faces eager to accept the challenge of obtaining a quality education. The Guests of Honor have arrived. Are you prepared to serve these elite members of society?

Michelle Whitehurst Goosby©September2008
THE GUESTS OF HONOR

My Mama

A TRIBUTE TO MY MOTHER

My Mama shares everything with me
And my brothers and sisters all the time.
A giving loving woman she is.
I told my sister just the other day,
"Mama is such a generous woman."
Then I thought to myself, "She has always been that way."

When I was little, My Mama sang to me and my brothers and sisters all the time. I remember those songs to this day. My Mama sang nursery rhymes to us too. I marveled in the sound of My Mama's voice. What better entertainment could a little girl ask for? It was wonderful. It was marvelous.

My Mama baked goodies for me too, and my brothers and sisters all the time. "Like cakes and candy, cookies and brownies, pies and tarts." She baked luscious layer cakes, homemade ones too. She let us lick the bowl, the spoon and the beaters. I can still taste the cake batter and the real sugar chocolate frosting. One slice was never enough. It was an insatiable experience to say the least. The anticipation of every bite was more than overwhelming. It was downright self righteous. We would all gather around mama in anticipation as she took the time to give us each a portion of her homemade motherly love. And every mouth watering bite melted in your mouth. I can see her spooning generous portions of that gooey-ooey-chewy delicacy for each of us, especially that freshly made caramel with chunks of pecans thrown into the mix.

"I'm talking about that chewy gooey drop dead delicious 'kinda' candy."

And no I didn't bring any of those delicacies with me today to share with you.So just pull yourself back together and listen to the rest of my story.

Like magic there it was, pecan and caramel and chocolate. I could barely wait to see that sticky delicacy all over my little fingers make its way to my big mouth. But not for long, in moments it was making its way down my throat. I can still see myself lick my fingers clean with no shame.

My Mama shares whatever she has with me and my brothers and sisters all the time. "Like that valentine candy Daddy always remembered to give My Mama on Valentine's Day." She would hold out that heart shaped box of luscious chocolates as we gathered around her in anticipation. I can still see the smile on her face as we eagerly picked out the piece of our choosing. She even gave us a second round. We lived for that moment. We would sit there together, Mama and me and my brothers and sisters all the time, indulging in chocolate and caramel heaven. And no she wasn't trying to promote tooth decay. So you can just get your mind out of the gutter.

We knew Mama would make her way into the kitchen preparing those delicacies with us in mind. She didn't do it just every now and then, but she did it for me and my brothers and sisters all the time. With a smile on her face she found it a pleasure to do the honors. And to think as the children of this loving woman, me and my brothers and sisters were entitled to this privilege all the time simply because she gave birth to us. You should be so lucky. What a blessing it is to have such a loving mother.

My Mama "ain't" just a cook either, she is a fighter too. And don't try to correct my English. If it was good enough for Sojourner Truth to say "ain't", it's good enough for me.

I remember how that sixth grade teacher who without looking at my records took one look at my black skin and immediately decided that I should be placed in the special reading class. My Mama set him straight right away by letting him know that I was a straight-A student. And later, my granny also told him so to his face. My mama had to fight all of her life. And she taught me and my brothers and sisters to protect ourselves all the time. She taught us to stand up for ourselves. To successfully pull that off you know you got to put on the armor of God.

All that "fightin" has made my mama a survivor. She's weathered many storms, raising five children, she and my daddy alone, working their fingers to the bones, struggling to put food in our mouths, clothes on our backs, and a roof over our heads. When the enemy stepped in with a vengeance, this Lady had to stand up to him and say, "Get thee behind me Satan." I'm talking about a mother who had to sit and watch helplessly as me and my baby sister suffered with life-threatening illnesses over which she had absolutely no control. She had to watch as me and my brothers and sisters made missteps, tripped, trumped, and took the wrong turns in life's journey. She then gleefully watched as we picked ourselves up, turned ourselves around and made the right turns, knowing all the while that it was God who had done the honors. She held on to God's unchanging hand then and she holds on to His hand even more tightly now. You've heard this story before. Do you know what it means to have a firm grip on the unchanging hand of the Master? It is an old story that unfolds time and time again in the life of a loving and devoted mother like My Mama.

You better not mess with My Mama either. She is the sole of strength. She "ain't" nobody's fool. You better not mess with her. You don't want the posse coming after you. You know who I'm talking about, My Daddy, number one. "Me and my brothers and sisters will follow suit with the 'grands' and 'greatgrands' tagging along."

My Mama is the most educated woman I know. I'm talking about life's education. When I think of my mama, I see a discernment that baffles the most brilliant of minds. She can take one look at you and know with certainty whether you are for the right or for the wrong. She has the memory of an elephant. "That lady don't forget nothin."

As I gaze at My Mama I see the epitome of pure womanhood wrapped in a blanket of gleaming blackness exuding a wisdom that only good genes, age and experience can produce. My Mama told me and my brothers and sisters all the time, "Feed people out of a long handle spoon." She'd say "You let them run their mouths and you run yo business." When she smelled a rat she'd say, "Somethin in the milk ain't clean." or , "Somethin's rotten in the cotton."

My Mama gives off this wave of generosity that serves to validate her, not just as a mother, but even more so as a humanitarian. She will give you her time and her last dime just to lift you up because your wellbeing has top priority in her life.

When My Mama is near, you better know an ever flowing stream of love fueled by dedication and devotion is not far behind. With a few dollars in one hand and a mountain of drive, determination, love and devotion in the other she cared for us, fought for us, shed tears for us, taught us right from wrong, loved and nurtured us.

My Mama's love just keeps on flowing and flowing and flowing through me and my brothers and sisters all the time. Fulfilling her duties as such is a pleasure and task that she takes seriously. I'm talking about a God fearing, Bible reading, praying, loving, beautiful, generous, caring, specimen handmade by the Lord Himself. I'm talking about My Mama.

Michelle Whitehurst Goosby© 2008
MY MAMA

In Full Bloom is the Rose!
A TRIBUTE TO SENIORS

You are the seasoned entrée at the table of life. When you look in the mirror, the face staring back at you is reminiscent of the blessings that God has bestowed upon you.

Oh yes, you have been around awhile and you thank God for the years He has given you. Those fine lines and wrinkles are nothing but a track record of your many gains and your few losses.

Oh Yes! You've got some miles on you, and rightly so. So you're getting older, much much older as you may see it. Your hair is thinning and graying. You don't move as swiftly as you use to. Sometimes you have to use your walking cane. Well, so be it! Thank God for the privilege. Your travels through life's journey have done you a great service. They have proven you to be the strong beautiful woman you are today.

When you look at your children, your grands and great-grands, you see yourself and you can't help but smile. You are drenched in God's grace and mercy. You are all wrapped up in His love. You are living your life, and a full one it has been thus far. You have seen much. You've been through much. What a story you have to tell. You have created a legacy without even knowing it.

You've climbed high Mountains, insurmountable, that make Mt. Everest, the highest mountain in the world, look like a molehill. Mt. Everest, echoing to the tune of 29,035 feet in height, can in no way, form or fashion compare to the mountains of life you constantly climb. I'm talking about living and doing it well. Sometimes on your merry way you had to put on your breaks and rest a little while. Because of the finder binders along the way, sometimes you had to put it in the shop for a few minor repairs, but nonetheless, you got right back on track, stronger than ever before. Heaven forbid, the fool who tries to get in your way. You better run for cover world if you dare try. The Master has just served notice, "The Senior Citizen has arrived!!" So move out of the way before you get run over. There's plenty of room for everybody. Don't fret! Your day just might be coming!

You've crossed vast Oceans that make The Pacific Ocean, the largest ocean in the world, look like that pond in your neighbor's backyard. The Pacific Ocean, encompassing 65.3 square million miles in area, and reaching a depth of 35,798 feet at its lowest point is no match for the oceans of life you repeatedly cross. I'm talking about wading in the water children while the waves toss you to and fro. You crossed that ocean and not by yourself. You went under many times but you came back up. There exists no tool that can measure the depth of your tribulations, the width of your trials and the height of your joy. Only the Lord can calculate that volume. Go have a little talk with Him. Tell Him all about your troubles and woes, your exhilaration and contentment. Living grounds this advice in stone. Ask any Christian.

You've earned a Wealth that makes the net worth of Oprah Winfrey and Bill Gates, two muti-billionaires walking the face of the earth today, look like a negative balance in a checking account. I'm talking about that aura of wisdom that precedes you every time you walk into a room. Everybody wants some of it. Put your check book back in your pocket. You can't buy wisdom. You've got to live to earn it. Those fine lines and wrinkles are nothing but a track record of your gains and losses. They serve as a map illustrating the routes you've taken as you walk this life. The Lord gave it to you and no man can take it away. Billions of dollars in pocket look like insufficient funds in the bank when you don't have the Lord on your side. Oh! The sweet scent of victory. It gets sweeter as each day passes by. Oh! The joy of living. You are beyond the shadow of a doubt, a wealthy person.

You've weathered Storms that caused you pain and stress that far exceeds the capability of any hurricane, tornado, tsunami, avalanche or the like. The devastation of Hurricane Katrina, a category 5 hurricane with wind speeds as high as 175 mph, is no match for the hurricanes that have made landfall in your clean heart. Your heart has been broken countless times in the past and you're still here. You've lost loved ones, you've been talked about, you've been lied on, you've been misunderstood, you've been looked down on, but as the Bible says, "No Weapon Formed Against Me Shall Prosper." You find solace in those words. And people on the outside have the nerve to wonder how you got back up. Ignorance is rampant.

Today, this is our tribute to SENIORS. We honor you. You've graced us with your wisdom. You are an inspiration to us all. We love you. We thank God for honoring us with your presence. Thanks be to God. Step aside world. In Full Bloom Is The Rose.

Michelle Whitehurst Goosby© 2008
IN FULL BLOOM IS THE ROSE

CHAPTER FIVE

Straight From The Heart. . .

A TRIBUTE TO MY PASTOR, DR. J. HENRY WILLIAMS AND FIRST LADY JANICE WILLIAMS

AIDEN ISAIAH

With the Key in Hand

With a thrust you're crossing the 13 year line.
With the key in hand, Oh how brilliant it shines.

With perseverance and strength, this mountain you climb.
Wrapped in God's armor for the harvest is nigh.

You stand for the Lord in good and bad times.
You waste not a moment. Ain't got time to whine.

You preach with a rigor, the Word intertwined.
Within each sermon, a message so fine.

You walk with a confidence dressed to the nines.
The First Lady concurs. She is so inclined.

I cannot imagine the nights you have cried.
How the day progresses, how high is the tide.

The morning cometh with joy, oh what a prize.
Growing closer to Jesus, you are the wise.

A new journey begins, God's Spirit presides.
With the key in hand, how brilliant it shines.

Michelle Whitehurst Goosby©August 2009
WITH THE KEY IN HAND

The Master Handpicks His Warriors

The Master said so in His Word
"I build My Church upon this Rock."
The Master handpicks His warriors.
Especially those who lead His flock.

Today we honor our trusted leader
Not just because it is the thing to do.
We honor someone close to our hearts
That special someone happens to be you.

May God continue to bless and keep you
As you guide and lead us day by day.
May He wrap His loving arms around you
As He keeps you from harm's way.

We want to thank you for being our pastor
As showers of love on you we rain.
Due to your leadership we are the better.
And our lives will never be the same.

Michelle Whitehurst Goosby©October8,2006
THE MASTER HAND PICKS HIS WARRIORS

The Music And Its Minister

IN MEMORY OF THE MINISTER OF MUSIC
BROTHER ALFRED BURNETTE

No matter how far we run, we cannot escape it.
No other tongue, to everyone, can claim to be as explicit.
Streaming through our boggled minds, we awaken with it.
On every end, there it is, Oh how exquisite.

Running through our being like a thread, tantalizing is it.
Fiery souls set instantaneously, as we eat, sleep, and breathe it.
Flowing smoothly like a constant stream,
every fiber immersed in it.
Rapids run through simultaneously, as
the Master walks us through it.

Through complete devotion that comes with it.
It's no wonder how blessed are we who live it.
Our Father's Church is a haven for it.
Though far and near, you will find it.

There is someone here who lives and breathes it.
This thing that touches those who hear and feel it.
Through his expertise, God delivers it.
We can't predict him. That's the work of the Spirit.

He gives us the tools we need to use it.
Spends countless hours with us going through it.
God works through him to ensure that we receive it.
As we see in his face how he lives and breathes it.

He tickles the ivories on Sunday morning.
And to one and all we give it.
He hits some awesome notes himself.
And inspires all those who hear it.

This someone gives us the chance to spread our wings.
For this very purpose, he was sent here to us.
See why we consider him such a beautiful thing.
We thank You for him, Heavenly Father, above us.

God speaks to us through the Music Ministry.
God gave us a messenger nobody could ever forget.
He delights us with its Grand Delivery.
The Minister of Music, BROTHER ALFRED BURNETTE!!!

Michelle Whitehurst Goosby©2005
Friendship Missionary Baptist Church Mass Choir
Dr. J Henry Williams, Pastor
Enterprise, AL 36330

To Such A Leader! To Such A Friend!

Everybody is in a frenzy
As the pastor's big day rolls around again.
We can't wait to pay tribute
To a such Leader! To such a Friend!
We hear him every Sunday morning
Speaking the Word from that pulpit.
Stepping on toe after toe,
He just won't quit.

"Ouch!" says the usher
Standing proudly behind the back row.
"Who told him what I did last night?
How could he possibly know?"

The deacon in humiliation thinks
"Oh Lord, how that hurts!
How did the pastor find out
I'm the one who's been slinging that dirt?"

In disgrace, the alto in the choir mutters
"I just want to hang my head.
One of those nosey sopranos
told him every mean thing I said."

"What!" yells the Sunday school teacher
"The word is out. I was such a fool."
"Running off to that other church!
Somebody told Pastor. And I wanna know who."

"He might think!" frowns the pew member.
"That I put church business in the streets."
"They were just innocent conversations."
"I hope he don't think I'm the leak."

All fun aside, let's get serious.
Pastor, your leadership we cannot buy.
For God is the source of all you give
And He does it in the twinkling of an eye.

Together we come to pay tribute
To someone who helps to keep us straight
By feeding us every Sunday Morning
God's Word on a silver plate.

He teaches us on Wednesday nights too
Although many of us fail to show up.
Then there are those of us who hear him
And still we leave with an empty cup.

There are those who show up for church mad.
It's written all over your face.
You ought to be spending time
Making the world a better place.

Why do we thank Jesus for such a leader
Who reminds us to stay on task?
Who doesn't mind speaking God's truth?
Do you even need to ask?

The answer is quite simple.
Church member, do you dare to say?
He feeds us every Sunday morning
With the Word to carry us on our way.

The Word is ours for the picking.
There is no excuse for indiscretion.
Read your Bible. Go to church.
Study your Sunday school lesson.

We Thank You Jesus for the Pastor.
We joyfully cry out time and time again.
Oh What an Honor To pay tribute
To such a Leader! To such a Friend!

Michelle Whitehurst Goosby©2008
TO SUCH A LEADER! TO SUCH A FRIEND!

CHAPTER SIX

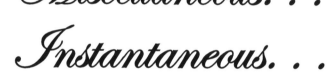

Miscellaneous. . .
Instantaneous. . .

JACQUELINE MICHELLE

Yes We Can!!

Economic Upset has the country
In such an unruly state.
Trim the fat. Cut down on the sugar.
Serve "Yes We Can!" on the dinner plate.
A new family in the White House
A new leader America takes.
An African American he happens to be.
Ain't nothing but icing on the cake.

Dehydration of the economy
I'm thirsty. Give me water.
Yet you beg me for a handout.
And I ain't got change for a quarter.

A heavy dose of "Yes We Can"
Served continuously everyday.
Obama prescribes, but don't forget,
God says, "Kneel Down and Pray."

A Congressman said so with a passion,
"They don't get it. These people are idiots."
Eighteen billion dollars in bonuses,
Using taxpayer's money to get it.

Recession, some say Depression.
"Gas prices up, Gas prices down."
"Pull up your sleeves." "There's work to be done."
"Yes We Can!" goes for another round.

"The economy shrank 3.8%
in 4th quarter of 2008."
"The challenges", he says, "we face are real."
"Yes We Can!" reiterates.

Japan embraces a new English teacher
And his best selling book.
The world looks on in admiration.
"Yes we can!" takes on another look.

Ice storm in Louisville
No power it seems in sight.
Hypothermia, carbon monoxide poisoning,
People fighting for their lives.

Smithsonian wants Queen Aretha's
Inaugural Bow Tied Wool Hat.
"Such a crowning moment in history," says she
"It will be hard to part with that."

I just lost my house. I just lost my job.
I just signed a loan subprime
My country reaches out a hand
God steps in right on time.

To this country I give my all, my best
The line of duty, I give my life.
My condition; Oh Lord, it preexists,
Health insurance, nowhere in sight.

The House, The Senate and little ole me
Republicans and Democrats
Bickering over what won't, what will
Yes We Can! is up to bat.

A train wreck in the making? Not so!
Get geared up for another round.
Don't even think of going there.
"Yes We Can!" has come to town.

When all is said and done, "I can't."
Executor of the crime,
Concedes as the humble "Yes We Can!"
Crosses the finish line.

Michelle Whitehurst Goosby©2009 YES WE CAN!

Art Cries As I'm

Art cries as I'm no longer bound for I'm
Standing in the midst of a golden mine.
It wraps its arms around you every time.
"It takes my breath away." says all mankind.
It warms the heart, soothes the mind.
Appears so clearly to the blind.
Like the taste of a sip of the finest wine.
Like Amazing Grace, every single line.

I stepped out of the doorway dressed to the nines
Met with the fresh scent of a tree called pine.
Overwhelmed with beauty at this point in time
Swept away by the breeze and radiant sunshine.

The butterfly floats; the bells they chime.
The artistry, Oh how it boggles the mind.
Stormy oceans I cross. High mountains I climb
All because of the Great One Who designed.

The fruit in the orchards, berries hanging from vines
To pick a few plump ones, I was inclined.
Apples and grapes, peaches and limes
Indulging in such glory ought to be a crime.

Then my attention is captured while I sit and dine
By a woman with needle and thread entwined.
Red, white and blue tapestry, I cannot decline
A craft patriotic, Art one of a kind.

I, then, turn and see Truth stand tall and refined
Neither read nor write could she at this time.
Mesmerized by a slave who spoke intense lines.
"Ain't I A Woman" I feel as I'm.

With brush in hand and strokes so fine
A woman of great age sparkles and shines.
Rich colors running up and down her spine
A waterfall of paintings in Grandma's prime

A child prodigy cometh, a man Art has assigned
With piano, harmonica and hearts sublime.
To make beautiful music that transcends the times
My Cherie Amour speaks the blind.

The course of my life, though roads may wind
Art cries as I'm no longer bound for I'm
In the midst of a journey, He has aligned.
I think of the Great One Who designed.

Michelle Whitehurst Goosby©March 2009
ART CRIES AS I'M

Bringing the Dead Back to Life

I stand here before a crowd,
A somber and morose cluster of fruit.
I've got to do something about this.
I promise you this mood won't last long.
I am on a mission. It is time to raise the dead.

Bringing the Dead back to Life
Healing the sick, mending the wounded heart
Lifting spirits with mere words.
That is my job.
That is my MO.

Bringing the Dead back to Life
It's not only what I say but how I say.
I get up before a crowd and I open my mouth.
These words come flowing out.
Not just any old words and not just any old way.
I've got to mold these words into a masterpiece.

Bringing the Dead back to Life
I want everyone who listens
to what flows out of my mouth
to have no regrets.
I want the hearer to anticipate coming back
because you've been hit by a tidal wave.

Will the dead rise tonight?
Do I have what it takes? Do I?
Will I lift the spirits of the souls?

Will the words I share paint a smile
or rain a storm amidst the masses?
Are they powerful enough to cause volcanoes to erupt?

Can I take simple words,
assemble them in such a way
to form a concoction that is medicine to the soul?
Not without the love of Jesus.
Case In Point!

Michelle Whitehurst Goosby©2008
BRINGING THE DEAD BACK TO LIFE

Oh Ye, The Great Inquisitor

I sit here patiently, so I thought, minding my own business.
On my best behavior, I quietly listen.
Never making a sound, drinking every word up
That others divulge.Lord knows this is tough.
Reserving judgment for later, being a good little girl
As the wheels in my brain spin out of this world.
All of sudden I am bombarded with reality.
I break dead silence as I enter actuality.
I began asking questions. That's my prerogative.
Flowing like a river come these words, interrogative.
What did he do? When did it happen? My goodness, what for?
I smile and think to myself, Oh Ye, The Great Inquisitor!

Michelle Whitehurst Goosby©January 27, 2007
OH YE, THE GREAT INQUISITOR

Poetically Inspired

Between Calculus and Physics
I'm spreading myself thin.
Every teacher wants a piece of me.
How can I possibly win?

World Literature, History
Chemistry, Biology
Give me liberty or Give me death!
That's my ideology.

Frustration has consumed me.
I can't see my way through.
I'm blinded by confusion.
Someone please tell me what to do.

Then a small voice from out of nowhere
Whispers gently in my ear.
Hold tightly my distressed one.
Be steadfast. Be of good cheer.

Take a journey to the Library.
Plan to spend quality time.
Pick up a good book, I tell you.
Read every line.

As you thumb through the shelves,
Make an inspiring selection.
Pull out a book of poetry.
You're sure to make a connection.

Take advice from these veterans,
Kipling, Kilmer, and Guest.
Cling to words, Oh so soothing.

They'll put your mind at rest.

Over there, Oh brave one,
There's Brooks, Wheatley, and Angelou.
After reading their words
You shall never let go.

Overwhelmed with bliss.
My journey has just begun.
What a revelation it is
To be having such fun.

I commission you my friend
To partake of my cup.
After one taste of this drink
You shall never get enough.

As I depart from this place
Free of confusion and despair,
I return to my studies
Ready to work, I declare!

Filled with a passion,
Poetically inspired,
Such beautiful poetry
Sets my soul on fire!

Michelle Whitehurst Goosby©March 2005
POETICALLY INSPIRED